HILARIOUSLY

FUNNY THINGS
TO DO WHILE
WAITING
FOR YOUR
COMPUTER...

by
TONI GOFFE

Dedicated to Tim, Tobin and Peter without whose
help....

First published in Great Britain by
Pendulum Gallery Press
56 Ackender Road, Alton, Hants GU34 IJS

HILARIOUSLY FUNNY THINGS TO DO WHILE
WAITING FOR YOUR COMPUTER..
ISBN 0-948912-35-9

Printed in Great Britain.

ABOUT THIS BOOK:

How many times have you sat in front of your computer **WAITING!** for it to complete a task..

      WAITING! and staring at the screen, while the minutes tick by, you could be doing something useful. But what? There's not enough time to actually **DO** anything, and by the time you've thought of something really, really good, the **WAITING!** has stopped, the task completed and you have to get back to work.
      If this is a problem that persists in your life, then **THIS IS THE BOOK FOR YOU!** It tells you how to fill in those precious, but now, sadly lost moments. But not just filling in time, helping it to pass, but filling it in constructively, inventively and creatively.
      As soon as your computer starts making you **WAIT!** pick up this book and open it anywhere and start reading. Then do what ever the item tells you to do!
      It will be great fun, and I'm sure, in some cases, change your life!

Work out how many minutes in a day you spend
WAITING-FOR-YOUR-COMPUTER! to
complete what ever task you've asked it to do for
you.....
Then work out how many hours of your life
you've spent waiting for a computer to get it's
act together.

Now work out how long it's going to take you to
get **YOUR** act together, and not be at the beck
and call of a machine that has nowhere near as
much brain power as you have, and compared to
you, is pathetic.
What can you do to rectify this?
Read on for the fascinating answer...........

Learn to Juggle: Pick up three items from your desk and throw them into the air, and try to juggle them. Obviously, it will take a little time and practice to become proficient. But remember, practice makes perfect!

Drumming: Practice drumming on your desk. Use your hands at first, later, you can buy some proper drum sticks. Try some rhythms that will get your colleagues' feet a-tapping

Take your pulse : Are you healthy? Normal
pulse rate is between 60-80 beats per minute.
Average 72.
If you're not sure how to do this, look it up in a
medical book. While you're looking things up
check out the diseases.
Are there any you **DON'T** have?

Combustion: In recent cases of spontaneous
human combustion only the smoking shoes and
part of the legs of the victims were all that was
found. If this happened to you, which of your
shoes would you like your legs to be found in?

Love: Think back to your first love affair. Do you remember that first sweaty fumbling kiss? Do you remember your first girl/boy friend. What do you think they are doing now?

Think of Numbers : What numbers came up to-day?
How many people did you see on your way to work to day? How many cars? Buses? Bicycles did you see today? Make a list. Pick out six. Put them on your next lottery ticket. Good luck!

Maddening: Is there someone in your office you cannot stand? Someone who drives you really MAD!? Well, close your eyes and forgive them, for they know not what they doeth.

Space: Is there a large space on your office wall? Think of what graffiti you could write on it. Think of who it could be about. Make a note to buy paint tonight after work.

Beauty Hint: Lay back in your chair with your head back, looking at the ceiling. Place two cucumber slices from your sandwiches on each of your now, closed eyes. This will relax your eyes, and take away that morning puffiness. If you have no cucumbers use old tea bags. Count slowly to 100.

Write down what your soon-to-be-famous last words are going to be.

Murder: Who do you think Jack the Ripper really was?   Make a list. Close your eyes and pick one.
Don't write Jack the Ripper! Although, he did know who did it!

Film: Think of the first film you ever saw. What was it about? Who was in it? Who took you? What did you drink? Did you have sandwiches? What was in them?

Television: When you were a child watching TV, who was your favourite character. Do a quick impersonation.

Game: Screw up some copy paper into a ball. Then "head it" into your waste paper bin or to an office colleague. See if you can start an office Head-the-screwed-up-copy-paper-into-your-waste-paper-bin game. Award points. Because........... points mean prizes!

Competition: You are in the **TV Chef of the year** competition final. Dream up your winning three course meal, and of course, the wine.

Mushroom: They say that life is too short to stuff a mushroom.
But you have the time, so what would you stuff it with? And how would you do it?

Chestnut: Have a chestnut about you. When a long **WAITING PERIOD!** starts, peal it clean. Even the bits in the groves. Show it to a friend.

Confusing: Take off your jacket, turn the sleeves inside out and put it on. Wear it like this until someone notices.

Joke: As someone is passing your desk, suddenly say "It's on your shoe!" Then as they struggle to see what they've stood on stare intently into a manual or similar. Deny that you spoke.

Stare intently at someone in your office. Keep staring at them until they suddenly notice something is going on. When they look in your direction turn away quickly, smiling secretly.

Crossword: Think of DOWNLOAD as the answer to a crossword clue. Now work out the clue with as few words as possible and without swearing.

Heads or Tails: Take a coin from your piggy bank and throw it up and catch it. Was it heads or tails? Using mathematical analysis of data using sampling techniques and probability theory, count how many times you have to throw it up before you can decide which comes up most, heads or tails.

Dice: Have some dice handy for moments like this. How many times do you have to throw the dice before double six comes up? If this becomes too loud and your colleagues find the noise of your screaming with delight too much for them, throw the dice into a padded drawer.

Question: If you could have one question that could be answered honestly, what would it be?
What really happened to the dinosaurs? What is the truth about Stonehenge? Where do I come from? Why am I here? When will I get a faster computer? When will I get a raise? How much will it be? Am I neglecting the spiritual side of life?

Clean out your wallet. Examine carefully every item. Show these to a nearby friend. Throw away everything you don't need. Make a note to do this more often. Fold it up and put it in your wallet.

Clean and file your nails. Dampen and push down your cuticles. Give yourself a full manicure. If you have time why not varnish them too. Hope they dry before the **computer finishes...**

Teleflower: Send a bunch of flowers to someone by phone as a random act of kindness.

Flowers: Send yourself a bunch of flowers by phone and sign it from some film or pop star, with the message
"Thanks for last night!" Be mysterious, and be sure you leave it on your desk where it can be seen.

Smoking: Decide to give up smoking. If you don't smoke, think about starting! It can't be more unhealthy than sitting in front of a computer all day **WAITING FOR IT TO FINISH!**. or what ever it thinks it's doing...

Lift: Can you lift up a chair by one leg from a kneeling position? Borrow a chair and try it. Get the whole office involved. Take bets. What about an inter-office league.

Morse Code: Learn the Morse code and get someone near you to learn too. Then in those dull **DOWNLOAD** moments bang out messages to each other, loudly on your desks.

Stranded: When you are famous and asked to appear on Desert Island Discs what will your eight favourite records be and what book would you take with you and what will be your luxury item?

Guilt: Check your pulse, now draw a police photofit drawing of yourself. Stick it on your computer screen. Are you feeling uneasy or guilty. Check your pulse again, is it speeding up yet?

Impersonation: Are you any good at impersonations? Do your favourite. Does anyone recognise who you are supposed to be doing? Don't give up the day job!

Drink: Dream up a new intoxicating drink. Put in it everything you can think of that you've ever enjoyed the taste of......Make one tonight!

Meditation: Sit back comfortably in your chair, close your eyes. Count backwards from 100 to 1 going deeper and deeper into a meditational mind level. Stay awhile and have fun. Count up from 1 to 100 to get back to normal. Open your eyes. Is anyone there?

Cookie: Think up a Chinese cookie slogan as good as "Help, I'm a prisoner in a Chinese cookie factory."

Write the corniest greeting card poem you can possibly think of and send it to someone you love. Trust me, you'll be surprised at what happens next.

Popular: Become popular in your office, take up a martial art. Develop a karate chop. Practice it daily, by repeatedly chopping the top of your desk with the sides of your hands till they become hardened. Hope you're still as popular.

Daydream... about where you'd most like to go on holiday, anywhere in the world. The Caribbean the Virgin Isles, or Martinique Now write down in your diary where you'll probably **HAVE** to go.

Phone Trick: On your mobile phone (you do have one don't you?) phone a friend and remind them that it's today that there's a large consignment of wet cement being delivered to their home.

Outrageous: Write down the most outrageous **chat-up-line** you've ever thought of to someone you **really** fancy.
Now promise sincerely that you'll say it to them at your next meeting.

Swimming: Take a deep breath and hold it for as long as possible. Time yourself. Now try this again, only hold your breath a little longer this time. Keep improving. Make a note to have some underwater fun next time you're in the public swimming pool. Can you swim a length underwater yet?

Haiku: Write a Japanese Haiku poem, using only seventeen syllables.

Pastime: Spin around 360% in your chair three times with your eyes closed. See if you stop where you started. In front of your screen, still **WAITING!** for that computer to finish!

Gardening: Clear a space on you desk for a Bonsai tree. Buy and start to cultivate it in your next break. You'll need some nail-scissors for trimming before the next **COMPUTER WAITING PERIOD**....

Arranging: Next time you're at the flower shop, why don't you buy some flower arranging items and when you get bored with your Bonsai tree (heaven forbid) you can change to flower-arranging.

Karate : Develop a karate punch and bring in some roof tiles to practice with. The next time you want to **smash your computer screen** just smash up some tiles instead. I'm sure your boss will understand...

Origami- is the art of folding paper into decorative shapes and designs. Make a paper plane and whiz it around your office to the delight of your office colleagues.

Winner!: When you win the Lottery what are you going to do with all that money? Write out a list of all your friends (including me) who you will make happy with a surprise million.

Tanka: if you had trouble with the Japanese Haiku poem try this. Tanka is a poem of 31 syllables.

Favourite: What are your favourite TV programmes? Write out what would be, your dream evening of viewing.

Lottery: Now, **WHAT** would you buy when you win the Lottery. Write out a list of all your **NEEDS** as a multi-millionaire. Personal jet planes are about £3,000,000. each, But if you want one with a private swimming pool, about £4,000,000. These prices are subject to alteration.

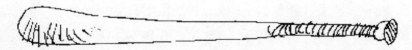

Frustrated: Do you get frustrated with your computer? Silly question I know.
Find something on your desk that you can hit, other than your £4,000 computer. While you're at it, find something you can hit it with, so not to injure your hands!

Shouting: When you are next shouting at your computer, try to be creative. Swearing at it is too easy, try and use this time to be inventive. I know it's hard in the heat of the moment....but....

" TECHNICAL DUSTBIN!" is good.

"OVERATED CALCULATOR!" is very good.

Can you better these?

Relax: Close your eyes and take a deep, deep breath. Relax and think of things that are far away and beautiful. Like desert islands, long white sandy beaches etc....

This is what to do when your computer wipes five weeks of intense work away in a flash of what only can be called malicious technical vindictiveness! Start again.

Enough!: If you've really had enough! You know what I mean. **ENOUGH!** Crawl under your computer desk and curl up into a tight little ball in the foetal position. Close your eyes and fists really tight and count to 1001 or just stay there until it all goes away.........

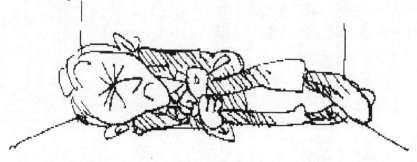

Mantra: A repeated word used in meditation to concentrate the mind. Think up one for yourself, Something to do with computers. Make a note of it and put it somewhere safe in case you forget it.

Manias: Obsession with or addicted to.....
Can you think of a good name for computer obsession or addiction? Try now...

Phobias: irrational or excessive fear of...
What about a name for
FEAR OF DOWNLOADING?

Collective Nouns: To express a number of individuals. Think of as many names as possible for a collection of fearful computer users who have a phobia of **WAITING FOR THEIR COMPUTER**.

Boats: How many types of boat can you name? This is not only a good exercise for the brain but very useful for when you do crosswords. We have 26, can you better that?

Card Trick: This will be a good time to practice a card trick.

Learn the "**Three Card Trick**" or "**Find The Lady**" as it is better known from a reliable magic book and practice it during **WAITING PERIODS**. Once perfected, you could earn yourself some money on the streets during lunch breaks.

Banana: If you take a packed lunch to work, amuse and amaze your work mates by peeling a banana to find that it is already cut into bite size pieces. You can do this the night before with a needle.
Don't give away the secret, even though your amazed work mates will pester you for an answer.

Answer: Take a needle and at the bite size areas push the needle into the banana and "cut" it, like they do in keyhole surgery. Continue down the banana.

Money Magic: Hold a bank-note lengthways and downward between your thumb and forefinger. Ask a colleague to put his same fingers either side of the note close but not touching. Tell him he can keep it if he can catch it. Then let go unexpectedly.
It is impossible to catch it! I hope!

Pub Trick: Practice this at your work-station to use later in the pub. Take a drinking partners drink and cover it with a clean handkerchief. Bet him that you can drink his drink **without touching the handkerchief.** Amid cries of "Impossible!" pretend to drink from a straw from the bottom of the outside of the glass.

"There, now pay up!" you say.

Of course, they won't believe you and remove the handkerchief to see. **Now**, quickly pickup his glass and drink it. You've won! **You** didn't touch the handkerchief, **he** did!

If there are calls of "sad" and "get a life" remember that all top magicians go through similar catcalling at the beginning of their careers. So persevere!

Card Trick: If anyone sends you a postcard of their holiday tell your colleagues that you can step through it. As the looks of amazement spreads across their faces fold and cut the card thus...first fold lengthways, cut along the folded edge leaving a quarter of an inch at either end, then cut thusly.....

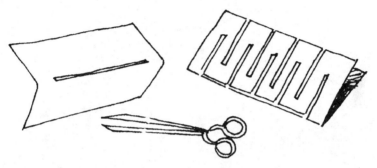

Open it out and you'll have a large circle of card that you step into and pull up over yourself. **You've stepped through the card!**

Sausage: This trick is probably best done on your own and not in front of your colleagues. It's called "Seeing the magic sausage". Hold your forefingers up in front of your eyes, horizontally and touching. Now, stare at the centre and slowly pull your fingers apart and magically a "sausage" will appear.

If you can't resist an audience, and who can, get your colleagues to try it too. Then when they make their discovery, you can say humorously

"You see, everyone has a sausage and remember, don't eat It!" Ha, Ha, Ha.

Write a limerick : ...about your office, the people in it, your computer, or your boss...
"There was an old man of.....

Design your dream car...what would it look like? What would it do? 300mph? Or gently fly you to work? What colour would it be? How many seats? Would they let down into a bed?
You little devil, You!

Unbendable Arm: Extend your arm out in front of you. Clench your fist and keep your arm as straight as possible. Ask a strong colleague to try and bend it. He should be able to do it easily.

Now, put your arm out in a relaxed way, imagine that your arm is a hose and water is gushing from it.

It should be impossible for anyone to bend it.

Immovable Hand: Place your hand on your head and hold it there. Ask your "strongman" to take it off. It should be impossible. You could even be lifted off the ground with your hand still there.

Lifting: Get your "Strongman" to stand in front of you and place his hands under your arm pits and lift you up. **Next time** he tries to lift you, place your hands lightly on his elbows. Lifting you up should be impossible.

Lifting a body: Sit someone in a chair, ask four colleagues to place their hands on the sitters head. **Gently** push down. Now, quickly get them to place their forefingers under the sitters arms and knees, and lift. It may take one or two tries, and it does work!

Dice Game: This could be dangerous and very exciting! The next time you have to make a decision about anything, write down six alternatives. Now number them. Throw the dice and what ever number comes up do that alternative. You can make this as dangerous and exciting as you can stand. Good luck!

Meditation: Sit comfortably and close your eyes, start repeating your **mantra.** Concentrate on your breathing. "Watch" the air flowing in and out of your nose. In your mind, go to your favourite beach and relax. Do this for twenty minutes, then open your eyes. Has your **COMPUTER COMPLETED ITS TASK?** Are people staring at you? Did your boss notice? Do you still have a job?

Yoga: The Lotus Position: Sit upright in your chair and lift your left foot up and place it on your right thigh. Now, lift your right foot up and place it on your left thigh. If you haven't tried this before you may find it impossible, if you do manage to get into it you may need help to get out of it. Lots of help!

If you do manage it, it is an excellent position from which to meditate. Don't fall off the chair!

Mind Body cleaning: Sit comfortably and close your eyes. Imagine you have a team of tiny but extremely energetic cleaners going through your body at a terrific speed, cleaning every nook and cranny as they go. Imagine them going down every one of your veins getting rid off all the cholesterol that has built up there. Now, in your lungs cleaning out all the tar. Open your eyes feeling wonderfully healthy and inwardly cleansed.

Headache Removal: The next time you find yourself shouting at your computer you'll probably get a headache.To get rid of it, Sit upright with your eyes closed and "look" at your headache. What size is it? What shape? And What colour? visualise the shape and decrease it by 25%. Make the colour lighter by 25%. Look at it again. Decrease it again by 25% Look at the colour again. Decrease it by 25% and so on till it has disappeared. The more severe it is the more you lessen the percentages. See if you can **disappear** your boss in the same way...

A COMPUTER TO SUPPORT

Retirement: I know you don't want to think about it, but in those
WAITING-FOR-YOUR-COMPUTER-MOMENTS.
I'm sure it must have crossed your mind sometimes.
What do you want to do when you retire? When do
you want to do it? Imagine what not having a computer to work with would be like. Do you have a pen-
sion plan yet? Should you get one? Have you enough
hobbies? Have you enough money? Are you putting
any aside? **Something to think about…..**

Money: Take out two ten pound notes or even better, borrow them if it's a Monday and you've had a heavy spending weekend. Fold them long ways and put the two heads together. Charles Dickens on top and the Queens' head on the bottom. The two together look a bit like John McEnroe the tennis player, don't you think? If you're not convinced try this, put them together the other way round and this surely looks like a circus bearded lady!

More Money: Look in your pockets for a 50 pence piece, the one with all the hands making a circle. Now look carefully at it, notice all the hands are large and heavy except one. That is supposed to be the Queens' hands. Not a lot of people know that...

Money Magic: Place two identical coins side by side on your desk, say, two ten pence pieces, with their edges touching. Now hold up a penny piece and tell your colleagues who ever can put the penny between the other two coins can have them!
Before you are crushed in the rush, add, that one ten pence piece must not be touched and the other cannot be moved! That will stop them in their tracks!

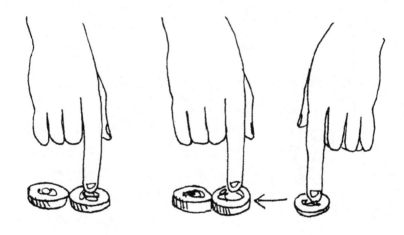

Answer: Hold one ten pence piece down with one finger and hold the penny piece down next to it in the same way with the other hand now pushing it along the surface of the desk, strike the ten pence piece! The remaining ten pence piece (the one that you can't touch) will be shunted away from the first coin leaving room for you to place the penny between them! This is bound to have your colleagues staring at you in utter amazement!

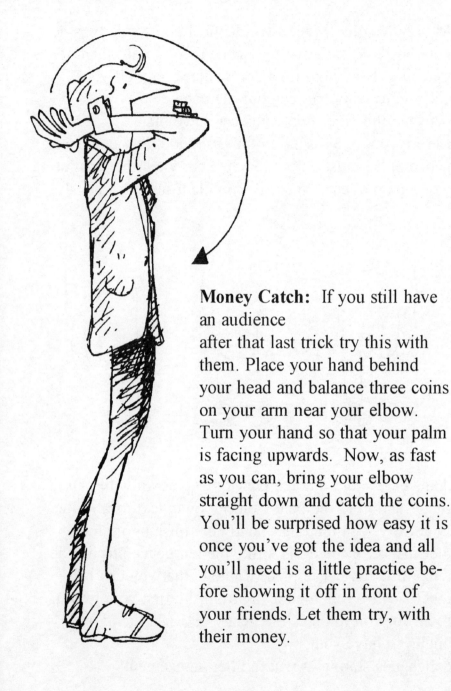

Money Catch: If you still have an audience
after that last trick try this with them. Place your hand behind your head and balance three coins on your arm near your elbow. Turn your hand so that your palm is facing upwards. Now, as fast as you can, bring your elbow straight down and catch the coins. You'll be surprised how easy it is once you've got the idea and all you'll need is a little practice before showing it off in front of your friends. Let them try, with their money.

Catching Money: When a visitor approaches your desk pretend to throw a coin in the air and catch it in a paper bag. Hand the paper bag to your visitor. When they look inside, **no coin!**

"How is this possible?" They will cry in admiration.

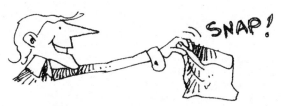

Answer: Hold the paper bag up with your thumb and your first two fingers. When you "catch" the coin, **snap** your fingers **on** the paper bag to make the coin-falling-in-the-paper-bag-sound.

Buy a number of paper bags for use when visitors approach your desk.

Pigeon: Taking about paper bags, here's a grizzly trick to upset your colleagues. **Producing a pigeon from a paper bag :** Blow up a paper bag and burst it with your hand. Feathers (which you have secreted in the bag before hand.) fly everywhere but no pigeon. Say something witty like.

"I must get this trick right soon, I'm running out of pigeons!" to get some hilarious laughter from your friends and some tears from the bird lovers....

Money: At your next
WAITING-FOR-YOUR-COMPUTER-MIND-WARP,
take some paper and make a list of all the money making
schemes you can think of, try and find a gap in the
market.

Doing this on a regular basis, you will eventually
come up with a really good idea that will make your
fortune. **Go for it!**

Thinking Ahead: On a piece of paper write out what
you want to happen this year in the areas of
career...money...health.... relationships...holidays etc...
Now, what do you want to happen in 2 years time...
5 years time...10 years time. Keep these lists
and review them every year.

Obituary: Write out your own obituary as it will appear in the papers at the end of your very successful life. List all your accomplishments over the years... your prizes...your incredible education.. your career moves...business successes... your fantastic relationships...etc.. etc...all that you are, at this moment, **planning.**

Goals: If you don't have a Goals list, this is the time to start one! Ask yourself this question... " What do I want?" When you have thought about it for a while and made a list, ask yourself **this** question. " What do I **really** want?" Make a list of the things you **really** want. Prioritise them till you have 10 really good ones. Write in great detail about each one. Then, what you can do to start attaining them.

UFO's: Have you ever had a Unidentified Flying Object experience? Or an Encounter of theThird Kind? Have you ever seen something in the sky that you couldn't explain? Or have you seen one and not told anyone for fear of being ridiculed? What do you think the **truth** is, are they **really out there** or **not?** Are they coming to get you at this moment?....
LOOK BEHIND YOU!!

Are You A Rat?... Or a Dog?...Or a Pig?
In the East you would introduce yourself by saying
"Pleased to meet you, I'm a Pig" They have a system
like our Zodiac Signs but they use animals. All their
birth signs are named after the twelve animals of the
Chinese Horoscope. It is worth studying as a guide to
who you should have as a business associate, lover or
marriage partner.

Aliens: Have you ever fantasised next about being
abducted by Aliens and taken to their flying saucer for
mysterious medical experiments? Take a few moments
to fantasise about what they would do with you during
the next **WAITING-FOR-YOUR-ALIEN-
COMPUTER...**

Learn French: These **WAITING!** moments would be ideal for learning a language. Use a Walkman cassette player and buy some language tapes for your next **sitting-in-front-of-your-computer-and-waiting interval.**

Study: If you have a Walkman cassette player you could study anything you wanted to while your computer is having all the fun **DOWNLOADING**. Find out what the possibilities are…

Try and convince a colleague that you are listening to a study tape when you are dancing on your desk with your eyes closed shouting **"YEAH!"**

Famous: "Everyone will be famous for 15 minutes" is a quote from the New York artist Andy Warhol. When your 15 minutes comes up.. When will it be? Where will it be? And what will you be doing? And With who?.. ..and is it being videod?

Design: What would your perfect house look like? Design the house you'll own when you're successful. Where will it be? By the sea? How many rooms? What sized pool? Write in detail everything about your house you can think of... add it to your **"goals"** list.

Hypnotic Regression: Many people, under hypnosis, seem to be able to describe their past lives in vivid detail. Have you ever tried? Who do you think you were many lives ago?

Coincidence: Have you ever had a simultaneous occurrence of causally unconnected events lately? They are great fun! You meet people you haven't seen for years. You find things you lost years ago. You suddenly meet your own double...
Why don't you have one today!

Water Divining: Have you ever tried it? Some people have a gift for it, perhaps you are one.
Make a Dowsing Rod from a freshly cut Y shaped tree twig. Walk about your office in a trance like state holding the Rod lightly but firmly in your hands bent outwards to get a reaction! You'll be surprised what you find!

Self-Hypnosis is practised today as a therapy. It can help you reduce stress, tension, losing weight and giving up smoking. Also it can help people to become more self- assertive. Make a note to buy a self- help tape to help you overcome your personal problems. Play it during those stressful **computer waiting moments.**
That's when you'll really need it!

Dreams: Can you remember the dream you had last night?

It's very difficult isn't it, as they seem to fade the moment you wake up. Sometimes you may have a flash of what you were dreaming about at a odd moment, but it seems the only way is to wake up and write it down. Make a note to have a good one tonight!

Have it analysed by an expert.

Problem Solving: If you have a problem that you've been struggling with for days and can't resolve, you can often trigger the answer by doing something physical like jogging, a long walk, swimming or taking a long bicycle ride. Something that takes your mind off your problem. Your sub-consciousness will often supply the answer in a flash appearing in your conscious mind when you least expect it!

Fantasy: Did you ever have an invisible childhood playmate? A six foot rabbit, or a teddy bear that could talk to, Someone you could share your inner most thoughts with, supporting you through distressing moments of frustration. Why not reinvent them to sit with you through your next
WAITING-FOR-YOUR-COMPUTER...PERIOD.

Frustration: In those moments of utter frustration with your computer, when you could throw it through the nearest window, try .. Jogging on the Spot! As fast as you can in a sudden burst of energy. The faster the better! Within a few seconds you will have forgotten what the problem was…

Popping: Another way of getting through a crisis with **your computer** is to walk quickly to the postal room and pick up a wad of **Bubble Wrap** hold it in both hands, enjoying the feel and warmth of the plastic. Now start to pop the bubbles slowly, enjoying the noise of the bubbles make. Sit with it at your desk, popping. Take it home with you to help you cope with the rush hour traffic. Pop while you watch TV. Take it to bed…

Abdominal Cramps: How is your stomach looking these days? Any sign of flab yet? Are your clothes feeling a little tight? It might be time to try a little toning up! Warm up first, then lay on your back for Abdominal Cramps.

Bend up your knees and lay back hands behind your head. Bend up from the waist to about 80% and hold for 1 second. Repeat as many times as you can without straining. Once is promising, twice, impressive, three times, unbelievable!

Bored? : Do you ever get those times where everything seems to be boring? You've tried everything to stay awake and make life interesting and you're still bored? Well good news! It's time for a **paper-clip sculpture**! Collect as many as you can from friends and colleagues in your office, clear your desk and start creating!

Party Piece: Do you have a Party Piece that you can perform at the drop of a hat? You should have by the time you finish this book! If you haven't, **NOW** is the time to drag up your hidden talents and work on your "**ACT**". What will you do?

Films: What film have you seen recently that was truly memorable? Who was in it? Who directed it? If you wanted to see another film that had the same director how would you find that out? How many times would you see it again? If you were the star in this film how many times would you see it then?

BANG

New Dress: If you see someone in a new dress or suit that you want to comment on across a crowded office, be careful how you do it. Did you know that if you mouth the words "colourful" at someone it looks like
"I love you." **Be warned**!

Sweets: What was your favourite sweet? Do they still make them? Discuss with a sweet-loving friend the qualities of Spangles...Lemon Sherbets...Liquorice Allsorts...etc...

Buy a mixed bag and hand out everyone's favourites or better still leave them on your desk to encourage visitors to your space.

Chocolate: Are you a chocoholic? Do you prefer milk or dark chocolate? Have you tried chocolate from Belgium or France? Do you prefer it? Are you getting hungry? Would you like some right now? Why not get some during the next break, take them back to a secret place, eat them and don't share them with anyone else. yum, yum!

Television: I don't know why, but chocolate reminds me of television. Can you remember any old TV theme songs? Think back to your childhood viewing, do you remember the theme music from Robinson Crusoe? The Persuaders? or Captain Scarlet? Start a office sing-along. Get out the paper handkerchiefs...

Soaps: Are you a TV soap fan? Who are you're favourites? Is there anyone else in your office who's a soap fan too? You can find out by dropping a soap stars name into a conversation and see if anyone dares to pick up on it...

Television: Are you a very keen watcher? How keen are you really? Make a copy of the TV page from your newspaper and then with a pen, draw a circle around your favourite programmes then a square around the ones you're not sure about but would like to try. Join them all up with a line and you'll be able to see quite easily where and when you'll have time for a snack or a space to make some tea. Apply to be **Viewer Of The Year.**

More Television: Some people believe that watching TV is unhealthy. If you believe this too why don't you **workout** while watching? You can practice this at your desk while **you know what** is going on with your computer. Abdominal Cramps, already mentioned in this book, would be ideal. As you lift your head up you will be able to see the screen. Press ups would be an excellent viewing exercise.

Jogging: Would be the best of all. You could practice at your desk watching the computer screen as you jog. Another idea would be to buy a circular bouncer, like a little trampoline, for your desk space. It would save your knee and ankle joints from wear and tear. Perfect!

Physical Mystery : Stand in a doorway and hold out your arms until the backs of your wrists are touching the door jams. Now push out as hard as you can for the count of 100 or for as long as you can possibly stand it.

Stand away from the doorway and let your arms relax against your sides. After a few seconds your arms will mysteriously start to rise outwards. Weird eh? A Physical Arm Raising Mystery!

More Physical Stuff : Do you remember, as a child, trying to pat your head while rubbing your stomach? Well it's time to see if your independence has improved since those days. Have a quick go when you think no one is watching.

Films : Are you a film fan? If so, do you remember any of these famous film actors lines like…..
" Make my day.." "I'll be back…" " Alrighty then.." "Come up and see me sometime.." "You dirty rat.." "We need a bigger boat…" Can you remember any of these? What are your own favourites? Think up some more and have an **office film quiz.**

Sausages : If the atmosphere in your office is getting a little to serious here's a game that I guarantee will get everyone to lighten up. When someone asks you a serious question just answer "Sausages!" it will mystify them at first, then I'm sure they'll start to find it amusing and after a few more questions with you still answering "Sausages!" they'll collapse in hysterics and soon everyone will be smiling with happiness and suddenly it will be a wonderful place to work and waiting for your computer will be fun and all's right with the world.

ABC :   When you're next at a loss to know what to do when you're **WAITING FOR YOUR COMPUTER** write down the letters of the alphabet on one side of a sheet of copy paper. Make a list of animals that begin with those letters. If your computer is still **doing it's thing**, try another subject e.g. flowers, names, towns countries etc...... or if that's too easy try **Last Letter Chain :** Write down the name of a country, town etc or whatever group you chose, then, using the last letter of the word you just used, write a new country etc...e.g.

Germany, Yugoslavia, Austria, America....etc..........

Last Word Chain : This game is better played with a group of people, it's just more fun! It's a little like the last one. The first player says a phrase or saying and the next player takes the last word and turns it into **another** phrase or saying...etc...e.g....Birds of a feather...feather your bed...bed time...time waits for no man....etc....

Yes/No : A popular TV game of the 60's now recently revised. You have to play this with a partner. During a conversation the players have to get the other to say "Yes or No" A forfeit could put an edge on the game. A money forfeit can put even more, SEX even more!. If you get really good at it apply to the TV station for an audition. Would you like that? Did you say **Yes?** Good luck!

Questions : The idea is that two players carry on a conversation using questions only, make no statements…e.g…

"What's your name?"
"Why do you want to know?"
"Are you going to tell me?"
"What will you do if I don't?"
"What do you think I'll do?"
"Can't you guess?"
"Yes!" **OUT!**

Talking : Working with computers can be lonely work, and if you've been doing it for a number of years you begin not to want to talk to people. If you really get "into it" you may start talking to your computer and then to **yourself.** If this becomes a problem keep repeating "I must not talk to myself, I must not talk to myself..." as you walk around. Soon someone will take you by the hand and lead you away to somewhere warm and cosy, away from all the stress and anxiety of computers....go with them...

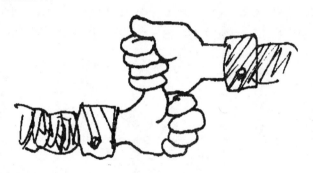

Physical Trick : Try this on a passing colleague, put one fist on top of the other and ask them to try and pull them apart. It should be easy. Now go into a trance-like state with as much theatrical flamboyance as you think the situation can stand, then present the fists again. This time they **cannot** prize them apart. How is this done? Easily really! As you put your fists together for the second time insert your bottom thumb into the fist above, without anyone seeing, of course and hold on tight. Your colleagues will be amazed at your new found strength and mind control. Flaunt it!

Only-I-Spy : In a lonely **download** moment write down a letter of the alphabet. Now look around your office until you find something that begins with that letter. Great! You win! If your computer hasn't finished it's task yet, you can extend the game by writing down the whole alphabet, cutting it up into letter size pieces and putting them in a drawer where you can take them out at a moments notice. Designate another drawer for use as a depository for used letters. Now it doesn't matter how long your **computer-waiting-period** is, you can just keep going from drawer to drawer and back again in an endless frenzy of fun.

Sitting : After sitting at your desk for an hour or two you must begin to feel the need for something physical. **Stretching** is excellent and I know you've tried **jogging** so now is the time for **Leap Frog!** Enroll some colleagues with the same predicament as yourself, line them up across the office and get jumping. Keep those heads tucked in!

Moody : When you find yourself fingering your bottom lip and wondering what do next during a **You-know-what period** and you don't really want to talk to anyone, try **Cards!** Have a pack handy for moments like this. Patience or Solitaire is the best card game to play by yourself. You probably have this game on your computer already, but, of course you can't play it, because **you-know-what-is-doing-you-know-what!** So you'll have to revert to the old fashioned way of playing with **real** cards.

Cards Continued : If you've had enough of playing with yourself and you want to enter into a noisy loud game with some friends try **Snap** and add to this game **Beat-Your-Neighbour-out-of-doors.** Similar cards for **Snap** and four for an Ace, three for a King, Two for a Queen and one for a Jack for **Beat-Your-Neighbour-Out-Of Doors.** Have a really **noisy card break!**

Noughts and Crosses : Probably, everyone knows this very old game also called **Tic-Tac-Toe.** If you can't find anyone in your office to play with you, you can always play with a telephone friend in another office. Number the squares thusly…and get on the phone!

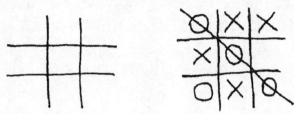

If this is too easy, what about…

Double Noughts and Crosses : This is a much more interesting development of the game. Start by sending your telephonic friend a grid like this…

To play, use either the whole frame or in one unit at a time. The winner is the one with the largest number of his symbol in vertical, horizontal or diagonal lines of three.

70

Grids : While we're in the grid mode, If your telephonic friend is still on the line why not revert back to that old school-time favourite **Battleships!** I bet you haven't played this for years! So lighten up and have another go! First draw four frames as below and send two to your friend.

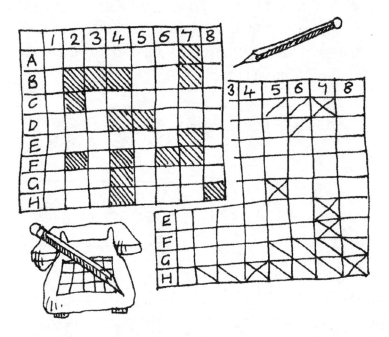

Shaded squares are Battleships of different sizes and the crosses in the other square are "Hits" and the diagonal lines "misses". Splice the main brace!

Codes : Have you ever wanted to be a spy? Here's the first step, the secret code! The cryptic message. Don't tell anyone, even under threat of torture. There are various codes in which your secret messages can be sent. The simplest is the two-line code. Write down the letters of the alphabet like this ...
ABCDEFGHIJKLMNOPQRSTUVWXYZ
ZYXWVUTSRQPONMLKJIHGFEDCBA...Write out your message and then substitute the letters to the ones below. Don't forget to give a copy of the code to the person you are sending it to...

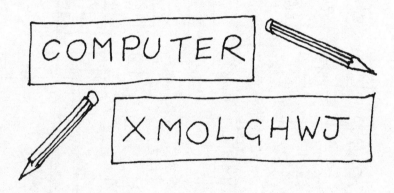

The Password Code : A more secret version of this type of code include a password or phrase as the bottom line e.g...
ABCDEFGHIJKLMNOPQRSTUVWXYZ
COMPUTERZYXWVSQNLKJIHGFDBA
be sure you don't repeat a letter...

The Rosecrucian Squares : First draw three noughts and crosses frames and then write in the alphabet thusly

A	B	C
D	E	F
G	H	I

J	K	L
M	N	O
P	Q	R

S	T	U
V	W	X
Y	Z	&

Instead of writing letters, you use a hieroglyphic of their position in the frames. e.g ...A is in the top left corner...
and is represented like this ⌐ N is in the middle of the second frame and so is thus ⟦··⟧ and Z is in the middle bottom of the third frame and so is represented like so... ⟦·.·⟧

In the **Rosecrucian Squares** the word **computer** would look like this...

You can make up your own codes and as complicated as you like. To make the **Rosecrucian Squares** code more complicated just start it in the middle of the alphabet somewhere.

Lunch :   The next time you have a lunch break really make the most of it. Have an office **Picnic!** This will take a little organisation, but it will be well worth the trouble. Prepare a hamper with the usual picnic stuff, knifes, forks, plates, paper napkins, salt, pepper and salt in little screws of paper, a tin opener and don't forget the bottle opener! And most of all, don't forget the **Food!** Salad cream, potato salad, Hard boiled eggs, and fruit etc. .etc…and a blanket to sit on, Now if you have your mind set on a particular day and it's raining and you can't go to the park., then set it up in a corner of the office, put some chairs around you for a little privacy. If the others won't join in with you, there's no shame in picnicing alone. They'll soon see the error of their ways and wish they had. Take no notice of their verbal abuse…

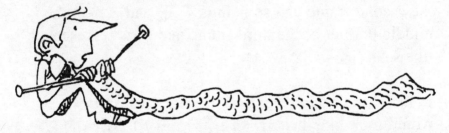

Pastime :   If you are eating alone take a book along with you to read in those awkward moments when you can't think would to do with your hands. Knitting is also a good pass time for moments like these…

Cooking : If you don't want to go through all the bother of getting a picnic together and you would prefer a snack, what about a **Bar-Be-Que**! You can purchase quite small ones that will easily fit on your desk and if you had a **Bar-Be-Que Pack** from a nearby supermarket you could have a wonderful meal in half an hour.

More Cooking : You can purchase small camping stoves that could be secreted away in a desk drawer. With this you could be really ambitious, but start in a small way before you get into entertaining twelve couples to a five course gourmet dinner. Why not start with **Pancakes?** You'll need ¼ lb flour,1 egg,1/2 pint of milk, salt, mixing bowl, wooden spoon, palette knife, and butter. Sift the flour into a the bowl with a pinch a salt. Make a hole in the flour and break the egg into it. Add the milk as you stir then beat into a batter. Pour batter into frying pan with the butter and Bingo! You're really to go! When you've eaten and you're getting a little full up, try tossing one and sticking it to the ceiling. You then forget about it, and suddenly it will renter the office orbit just when you're feeling a little peckish!

Desk Top : If you find you're spending more and more time on your own at this period of your life remember that nothing in life is permanent, things will change. But this might be the right time to start your own **Model Railway!** Clear away some of the junk from the top of your desk and start building an area for your railway. Stick down some green baize on your desk top and roll up some copy paper into balls, lightly stick them together for "hills", cover with papier maché and colour. Buy some track and rolling stock. You can make your own station from cardboard but buying it would be more presentable. Have a good look through a model railway catalogue for trees, buildings, people, animals etc...

Once you get it working you'll be the envy of your colleagues, well, the male ones anyway, get them involved in **shunting in the goods yard** and **train time tables.**
Dressing up as station staff just adds to the fun!
Don't forget your flag and whistle!

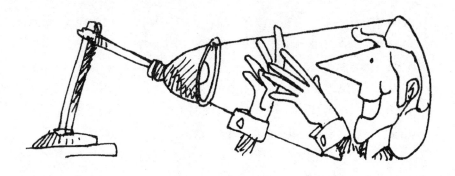

Hand Shadows : This will only work well if you can somehow black out your office windows. Imagine the surprised looks on your colleagues faces when they enter the office in the morning expecting to start a day of working and **waiting on their computers** but instead they are treated to an exciting Hand Shadow show, where your skills in the ancient Chinese art of Shadow Theatre are shown off in the best possible light. Here's some ideas to start you off...

Make sure you have a bright light to perform in front of so that the images will appear in sharp silhouette, to the wonderous delight of your colleagues.

Hand Puppet : If you really don't have enough room on your desk for a model railway then try a
Hand Puppet that you can hide in a drawer and bring out at moments notice when colleagues need a good laugh to cheer them up. If you choose to make one yourself, it's like creating a friend as you work..
You'll need a toilet roll, newspaper, scissors, needle and cotton, paint, ribbon and some material.

Cut the toilet roll to the length of your middle finger, roll a newspaper up into a ball. Put the ball into a square of the material and stick it onto the end of the roll. Paint a face on the "head". Fold the rest of the material in two, place your hand on it and cut out the "body". Sew around the edges and your ready to **GO!** Don't forget your **Gottle of Geer!**

More Puppets : I'm sure that your hand puppet was a great success and gave great enjoyment to your office colleagues. I can almost hear the laughter echoing around your office from here. As it was such a success what is the next step? Well **A Puppet Theatre**, of course! You'll need glue, some doweling, wire, eleven old cereal packets, cardboard, curtain material, newspaper, flour paste and some old photographs for backgrounds. Glue the cereal packets together as shown, cut and sew the material into theatre curtains and decorate with pasted photographs. Now the show can begin! I bet you can't wait to see the looks on the faces of your colleagues when you put your **Puppet Theatre** on your desk. There's no business like show business!

Wet Afternoons : What to do on wet afternoons? They're not a lot of fun are they? You should have dried out and read your newspaper by now so why not make a **newspaper suit?** You might need two or three newspapers, so have a rummage around the office until you have enough so you can get on with the cutting out and pinning and not bother anyone else till you've finished. On second thoughts you might need a pal to help you with the pinning, not easy by yourself, partially around the back, so enlist a helper. Someone sensitive to your situation, picking someone not on your wavelength will only spoil the enjoyment for you and the others.

Newspaper : If you have any newspaper over after your **suit making** roll it into a ball for a game of **Piggy-in-The-Middle.** Can be great fun on a wet afternoon if you pick the right person to be **Piggy**. Don't pick someone who doesn't want to play, they can spoil a good game. **BUT**, if you have used all the newspaper up, why not just pick up something personal off someone's desk, like a handbag or their shopping or their Filofacts, they'll soon want to join in.

Match sticks : Another occupation for a wet afternoons
is **Match Stick Models**. If you don't have a lot of room
on your desk for large models, like a cathedral or railway
station go for a **Match Stick Tower!** These don't take
up much desk space so you won't have to move a lot of
work stuff. You'll need some glue and, of course, some
matches. Use used ones, that's very important, I've had
and seen some spectacular disasters in offices when some
innocent beginner has set his match stick model alight
because they had forgotten to use used match sticks. In
my case it was deliberate vandalism as I **was** using used
matches at the time but I don't want to think about it at
the moment.

Window : Are you lucky enough to be working at a window? If so, why not build a **Nesting Box!** They can attract breeding birds to your office and give everyone a valuable opportunity for a little bird-watching.
To make a box that a bird will use you must be sure that it is firmly secured, weather-proof, and safe from attack by cats or insensitive office colleagues.

Follow the plans and put it together carefully. Don't leave screws or nails sticking out. Let's hope you attract a bird with your efforts. If you look after it you may have formed a relationship that could last for years.
That's if you still work there after this!

Garden : Everyone wants a garden, but not everyone has one. If you don't have one where you live then have one at your office. I mean a **Bottle Garden.** Purchase a large balloon-shaped bottle from a wine merchant and drag it to your office. Stand it somewhere where it will get plenty of light, but not in direct sunlight. Put a layer of small washed pebbles at the bottom of the bottle. Then cover the pebbles with 4-5 inches of sterilised soil from a garden centre.

The most suitable plants to grow in bottles are the ones that like a humid atmosphere like begonias, zebrinas, or maidenhair ferns and you can grow them all together at the same time.

You can make your own bottle garden tools from old spoons and forks from the canteen tied to long sturdy sticks. When you've planted your plants, water them thoroughly to make the soil damp but not swimming in water. Put the cork in and you wont have to water too often..
Turn the bottle occasionally to get all round growth.
Happy gardening!

Decoration: Is your computer an uninteresting grey colour? Then why don't you decorate it by painting flowers on it? Use as many different colours as possible, cover that boring grey completely. Lend your paints to your colleagues to make your office into a paradise of colourful splendour. Your bosses will probably want their computers painted too....

More Decorating : While you're in decorating mode, why don't you brighten up your whole working area? Balloons are fun! Streamers, flags, yellow " Post it" paper decorations, cuddly toys and flowers! If you are painting your computer, why not paint your desk or! work station, while you're at it? tell your colleagues!

Magnify : Have a large magnifying glass handy for those **WAITING-FOR-YOUR-COMPUTER** moments and really get into examining yourself. Look at your hands as you've never looked at them before. When did you last give your face a good looking over? Get a mirror and get going...

Happy? : Have a good look at yourself, hold up two mirrors to get an all round view. Could any part of you be improved by cosmetic surgery? Which Part? Make a drawing of how you would like to look. Start a cosmetic-fund for yourself.....or not.

New! : When you buy something new, always look at it through a large magnifying glass, in as much detail as possible. Don't leave any part of it unexamined. It somehow helps to compensate for the money you've spent on it, **Hopefully...**

Garden : Draw a plan of your ideal garden. Layout your office as your garden is going to be, using the chairs as your path and the desks as flower beds. Three drawer files could be the trees. Invite your colleagues to walk around it with you.

Flowers : Do flowers grow better if you talk to them? Some people are convinced that they do. Buy two potted plants and only talk to one of them. Tell your colleagues not to talk to the same one but they can talk to the one you talk to. I'm sure they'll be fascinated in this interesting experiment.

Sirsasana: The yogi head stand, very beneficial to the body and mind. Practice this on your chair by putting your head on your chair seat with your hands behind your head and your back against the back rest. Jump your feet into the air to the head stand position. This may sound dangerous. It is, forget it!

Copy: Make a copy of your face on the office copier and exhibit it on your desk. Tell people that is what you looked like before your cosmetic surgery. They will tell you how **handsome** you are looking now.

Model: Make a plasticine model of your boss and do nice things to it. He will change his valuation of you very soon, and even begin to like you.

Decorations; Fold your newspaper into a 6 inch shape and begin cutting into it making figures holding hands. Decorate your desk with the pulled out strips. If you have any over, decorate a colleagues desk while they are momentarily away.

Foreign;   Pretend to be foreign for a day. Don't answer any questions, pretend you don't understand. Talk in gibberish, make up your own language. Keep it up for the whole day. When you come in tomorrow you can reminisce about what hilarious fun it all was.

Stress: I expect you'll be chewing gum, because of your nerves. If not, you should try it, it's very healthy for your jaw to get that much exercise and very pleasant for your colleagues not to have you talking for a while. When the gum is finished try throwing it up and sticking it to the ceiling. Great fun!

Record: Have you ever wanted to be in the **Guinness Book of Records?** Think of what you'd do to get in it. The easiest way is to think of something new that no one has tried before. What about the biggest paper-clip sculpture or the highest building anyone has ever dropped a computer from. Can you better that?

Astral Travel: Have you ever had an out-of-body experience? Well now is the time to have one! These experiences mostly happen during near-death situations e.g. in hospital operating theatres, or **waiting at your computer**.....But some people can just will themselves into one. Try it, and if you are successful, why not indulge in some **Astral Travel** and visit a near-by planet.

Friends: There can be lonely times sat at your desk, when you crave the company of something other than human beings, well, adopt an insect. Ants are fun! You can keep them crawling over your hands for hours. Or spiders, crawl under your desk and look for one. Make friends, bring it live flies to eat. Talk to it and be the envy of your friends....

More Stress: If you suffer from high blood pressure and stress which, if you work with computers, you most certainly will, try this interesting way to lower it and become more relaxed. It is to experience **Animal Bonding !** Cats and dogs are good! Fish are better! Watching fish swim in a bowl on your office desk can be as relaxing as Yogic Meditation.

Pets: Take a pet to work with you tomorrow. Pets are very relaxing to be with and everybody will love them. That's if you remember to house-train them first. Cats and dogs are most fun, chasing each other round the office chairs, or something a little more re-laxing would be, as we have said, fish. But if you want something highly exotic to impress your office colleagues what about a Giant African Cockroach or a Vietnam Pot Bellied Pig!

Telepathy: Look around your office and pick out someone you'd like to have Telepathic Communication with. Close your eyes and send them a message. The nearer you are to a dream-like state the better, so late afternoon would be an ideal time to try this. Did it work? Don't give up! Write your message on a large card and stare at it now try to send it again.

Gravity: Have you ever thought much about Gravity? How and why it works? Could you defy it if you had enough willpower? You could suddenly float around your office giving everyone a nasty surprise.
Think how useful that would be during rush hour. Levitating at parties could make you very popular. Try it!

Kim's Game: Arrange some items on your desk and stare at them. Try to memorise them. Now make a list of what you remember. Did you remember everything? Did you remember **anything**? Can you remember why you are doing this? What is your name?

Remote Viewing: Travelling, in your mind, to a location and being able to give an accurate description of what is there. Do you possess this phenomenon? Give it a go! Take a map of, say, where you want to go on holiday. Go there in your mind and see if you like it.
How far is it to the beach? Check the travel brochure. Experiment by using a map of your immediate area, find somewhere you've never been before, go there, and describe it.
Then, check it out during your next break. This could be fun! Think of the possibilities!

Back Massage: Walk around your office and notice if there is someone who looks more tense and stressed than the others. Sneak up behind them and give them a sudden surprise back massage, they'll love it!

Draw a square, a rectangle, a triangle, a circle and a snake-like shape. Pick out the one that appeals to you most.

Geometric Anatomization: If you picked a rectangle, you are in a state of change. A square means you love detail. A triangle means you are a dominant achiever. A circle means you are a people manager and if you picked the snake-shape you're one of life's crazy weirdoes likely to be creative. Apply these findings to your job, are you in the right one?

When **WAITING-FOR-YOUR COMPUTER** becomes **utterly unbearable,** close your eyes and "enter" your computer in your mind. Walk around enjoying the inside, listening to the electric pluses sending messages to one another, all for **your** benefit.

Your computer is doing it's best just for **you,** it must be **love**. Your computer **loves** you, and you must learn to **love** your computer back.

Experience **COMPUTER-BONDING!**

Now, sitting at your desk **WAITING-FOR-YOUR-COMPUTER** to complete it's task will become something you'll be eagerly looking forward to...enjoy..

Disclaimer : We hope you will read all the items in this book with the intent to try them all. Now this might not be appreciated by everyone in your office that does not possess your advanced sense of humour. Particularly those above you. So it's up to you to gauge whether or not your actions will be acceptable, you might be risking your job. We did, and we lost ours, which is why we have time to write this book!